Up's and Down's of My Life

An Emotional Journey

Linda May Westbrook &

About Me &
Forward by Linda May Westbrook

Note to readers: Trigger warnings ahead for sexual abuse, neglect, invalidation, and self harm. Please read with care, and put your mental health first.

Poetry begins on page 9.

I was abused most of my life. It started when I was about five years old by my uncle. At the age I thought it was okay because he was an adult, so I did not tell anyone what my uncle was doing to me. When I was in grade four or five, I told my sister what my uncle was doing to me. My sister told me to tell my teacher and that my teacher could help me. The next day I told my teacher that my uncle was touching my privates. After she told me that he should not be touching my privets, she told me that it is not my fault and that she had to tell someone from family services. She called family services and a worker came to talk to me. The worker took me aside and asked me a bunch of questions about my uncle and if I knew the differences between good and bad touch. At this time I did because I learned about it a day or so before. I told the worker yes and I told her about what my uncle was doing to me. She asked me how long he has been touching me, I could not remember at the time. After school when I got home the worker was talking to my mom and dad about what I told her and asked my parents to keep him away from me, they agreed.

About a month later my uncle started to come over again all most every night to play cards with my mom and dad. They watched him for about a week. After that he started to touch me again. I never told anyone for about a year later. I found relief by hurting myself any way I could. I told my grade six teacher only because she was reading a book about a little girl who was being abused and I started to cry. When the recess bell rang, she asked me to stay in so she could talk to me about why I was crying. I told her because my uncle was touching me. She told me that it was not my fault and that he should know better. She called family services and another worker came to talk to me. I told the worker he was touching my privates. She took some notes and said she will be coming to my house to speak with my parents. She came over just after school and told my mom what I said and to not let him back in the home. Well my mom was very upset and told the worker she would. My uncle stayed away for about a week, after that week he started to touch me again.

By this time, I was hurting myself more almost daily. Another year went by and my uncle was still touching me. I was in junior high school. One day a teacher caught me cutting myself with a piece of glass. The teacher told the school councillor and he called me into his office. At the time I did not know why he called me in. When I got into his office, he asked to see my arms. At first, I said no. He said that he was told that I was cutting myself with a piece of glass, and that he just wanted to make sure that the cuts were not deep. So, I showed him my arm. He cleaned my arms and asked me why I did this? I told him because I can. I did not tell him what my uncle was doing. I was caught a few more times hurting myself and I told him the same thing, because I can. I finally told a teacher why I was hurting myself. She asked why I did not tell anyone. I told her that I have told someone twice already and they tried to help me and that they called family services. She told me she had to call them too because it was the law and she had to call them.

So, she called, and another worker came. I told her what I told the teacher. The worker said she would be coming to my home to talk to my parents. When she told them what I told her they got mad. The worker said they needed to keep him away or she was going to take my little sister and me away. My mom said that she was not going to stop him from coming over and the worker said that she was taking my little sister and me away. The worker left to call the cops. While she was gone my mom and dad were yelling at me, asking me why I was lying, or why I did not tell them. About a half hour later the worker came and took my little sister and me away. My sister and I were placed in care for about a week. We were returned home, and my uncle was not charged for what he did to me, and when he came over, I left the house. That was the end of him abusing me.

When I was 13 my cousin was babysitting me one day because my mom had to get errands done, so he and I sat and watched hockey as he cooked ribs. In between checking on the ribs he started to tickle me and it made me laugh. Then he moved his hand down and the abuse began again, this time with my cousin. Because of the earlier abuse it felt really good. Part of me wanted to go to his bedroom when he asked. I was just about to say yes when his phone rang. It was my mother saying she was home and to send me home if wanted to go. I told my bus driver about what happened, and the family services came and told my mom. My mom told my dad and my dad told him never to come near me again. He never came over again.

When I was 13 in a half, I had a boyfriend. He was in his 20's. He too was abusive towards me. I used to hide the bruise on my legs. He got me into smoking weed, drinking alcohol, and took my virginity away. At 14 I was hurting myself to deal with what had happened to me growing up.

Two months before my 15th birthday I was placed in an institution for children with mental health problems it was called C.P.R.I. While I was there I stopped hurting myself. I learned a new way to release my feelings. I learned to write poems. While I was in C.P.R.I my parents separated, and I blamed myself for it. To this day I still blame myself.

When I was released from C.P.R.I I was put into an all girl group home for about six months. I went to court a lot and the last time I went the judge asked me if I wanted to stay at the home or go back to my mom's. I went home. When I returned home things were going okay for the first two weeks, then things started up between my mother and I. When the workers from the group home came for the 3 month check in, I asked them afterwards, hoping I was out of ear range, if it was too late to change my mind and go back with them. I got into a fight with my mom and ran away to a friend's house.

I ended up dating her boyfriend. He was about 15 years older than me. A couple of months later I got pregnant. I was 16 and a high school dropout. I got married to the father because I thought it was the right thing to do. On Jan. 27, 1997 I gave birth to my daughter Evelyn. After my daughter was born family services came to the hospital and took her away. They said it was because I was involved with abuse when I was growing up and that I had a learning disability. They also said it was because of my mental health.

After I got out of the hospital, I noticed that my husband's attitude toward me has changed. He started to abuse me. He was forcing himself on me and had his way with me. While I was fighting for custody of my daughter, I started to see a psychologist. I left my husband about a year or so later, and I went to live in a group home for people that had mental health problems.

While I was living there, I met someone around my own age. I thought, *hey he's close to my age, so he won't hurt me.* I was wrong. He started hitting me. Writing poems had stopped helping me by this point, and I was back to hurting myself. With all this happening I lost custody of my daughter. She became a ward of the state.

Losing her had put me over the edge. I started to cut myself daily. About a few months or so after I lost my daughter, I moved out of the group home. I was admitted to the hospital a lot of times because of hurting myself. About a year later I left my boyfriend and went back to my husband, because I thought he changed. He was good to me for about a week or two than he started force himself on me again. He also started to emotionally abuse me. I told myself that I deserved it because I lost our child. I started to not care what happened to me or whether I lived or died. I couldn't care less. I stopped feeling emotions all together. I left my husband a few more times.

In late 2002 I found out that I was pregnant again. On June 20, 2003 I gave birth to my daughter Faith. While I was pregnant, I left my husband for the last time and I changed my life around hoping that I could keep my daughter. My daughter was taken from me. I still had contact with my husband only because he was the father. On two occasions he raped me again. These two times were different from all the other times. He had me by my throat. I was scared to even move. I finally got enough courage to charge him. I got the courage from thinking of my two daughters.

I lost my youngest daughter to Crown Worship in 2004 for the same reason I lost my oldest daughter.

In November 2003 I met someone and he's really good to me. He helped me through losing my daughter and through the death of my grandmother. We have been together almost two years now and all is good. He knows about what happened to me since I was a child and he is helping me to move on. I still have mental health problems because of my losses and my childhood trauma. I also can't have children anymore.

About hurting myself? I still do think about it, and sometimes want to act on that feeling, but I have not yet. The only thing stopping me is my boyfriend and my friends. My boyfriend is always encouraging me to write. He loves my writing, even the ones that are upsetting. He treats my poems as if I were writing in a diary. He won't read them unless I say it's okay. I love to write. It helps me in so many ways. I still see my psychologist. Sometimes I see him once a week, or every other week, and sometimes just once a month. It all depends on how I am doing. Every so often I show him one of my poems, so he knows how I am doing.

In 2017 I met my oldest daughter, Evelyn. I am a grandmother now.

I learned through my journey that all these things going on has split me into many parts. I am not just one voice anymore. I never was. We have Dissociative Identity Disorder. Here are some of the poems that we have written over the years.

The Poetry of Linda May &

My voice is sometimes not heard by the ones I need to hear,

A whisper is all I let out but a scream from within,

Need to learn talk instead,

Of whisper,

For only then the ones I need to hear,

Will hear my call,

But for now if a whisper is heard,

Then it is I that it came from.

Something Black, Something Yellow

September 19, 1995
Age 15

Part of me is in the black.
I need someone to talk to and that will listen and
    understand me,
And believe me.
But I have not found that someone.
The other part of me is happy full of love, but I need all of
    me to,
Be really yellow until that time comes I'll be bouncing off
    the walls.
To one part of me to the other,
But to come whole I need that person to talk to.
I wish that person was here so I won't have to go back to
    black.
Right now I'm in the black,
And I need OUT.

The Voice
September 20, 1995

As I walk through the halls I hear her voice,
I turn around and no one is there.
I turned around to start walking again.
And her voice I here again,
But this time,
I keep on walking.

The Voice II
September 21, 1995

I heard her voice again as I came back to school.
But this time it was more powerful.
And it was louder I could hear it more clearly.
It was saying run the way is yours.

No Tongue
September 29, 1995

As the day goes by I feel a change within myself.
But I go on, the world goes on.
It feels that I have no tongue.
I want to talk, but I stay silent.
The devil is within me it feels.
I need to get him out I need someone to sit down and
        read or,
Talk about the Lord,
But who?

Silence
March 23, 1995

As I get a chill up my spine, my eyes fill with tears.
I cannot bring it out in the open I will lose all I have that
        matters,
To me.
My true feelings are out.

The Fire
March 21, 1996
Age 16

As the sun goes down the fire in my soul burns,
Burns from all the caring and loving of friends,
I have found people who care for me,
And all that caring makes my soul burn of fire,
The fire will burn until no one cares.

Dream
March 20, 1996

As the night gets dark and colder, my heart and,
Soul gets weaker. Tried as can be but don't,
Want to sleep. Dreamland scares my mind.
Dreams turn into nightmares,
And nightmares scare me.
They get worse and worse every night.
I close this poem with a rhyme.

1-2 nightmares coming for me
3-4 better lock my door
5-6 better crucifixes
7-8 stay up late
9-10 never sleep again

Path to Freedom
April 8, 1996

As I sit here the path of freedom gets further away.
I use to be able to knock on the door,
But now and forever it's,
Back in another life or another world.
Well the way I feel right now is totally in the wrong path.
I have relived the pass,
Rof eht tsal emit.
(*This is how it's written down, but it says for the last time.*)

Foolish
May 18, 1996

When I look up into the sky and the clouds are flying by,
I wonder why men and women are so foolish.
They take nothing for granted but our selves.
There's a lot more out there in this world than ourselves;
Animals, children, air.

Loretta
July 26, 1996

As I pray tonight I think of you.
I wonder where you are and how you are.
We were so happy together but now we are apart.
We were like mother and daughter our love was great.
I pray hoping that we will be together again.

Love
August 25, 1996

Someone I know asked me if I knew what real love is.
I said no, not really.
She said, I think love is understanding, a commitment,
        and
Loyalty, and fun.
I said,
"Ya that sounds right."
She said that she would fall in love before I do.
She did,
But I got married first.

I am grateful
September 10, 1996

I am grateful for thee child in my womb.
I am grateful for the breath that I take.
I am grateful for my lover my friend.

I am grateful that our lord crated life.
I am grateful for the help of others.
I am tired for I am weak.
I am grateful for the strength to carry on.

Thee child in my womb brings joy and happiness.
The life inside of me has a healthy heart beat.

Fire in My Soul
March 30, 1997
Age 17

The fire in my soul is burning out of control.
The fire gets hotter and hotter as the days go by.
It scares me to let it out!
So I hold it back.
Knowing that I am hurting the ones I love, I do not want to
    hurt,
Them but I must hold back.
The fire is getting hotter and burns a whole in my soul.
I hope that I can put it out for good.
The fire in my soul is getting stronger each day I hide it
    by,
Getting hyper.
I must not let it out.
So I hold it back longer than I ever could.
I've tried everything I know to stay calm and in control,
I've tried all my friends' ideas,
But my anger comes back twice as bad.
I will hold back until I no longer can.
But let it out little by little till it's gone.

Anger

January 18, 1999
Age 18

My anger is erecting.
I can't control my anger no more.
Everyone with us for the past two years have seem to
    give up on,
Me, who wouldn't I would, but the bitch in me is out with
    my,
Anger, if someone says the wrong thing to me watch out.
I've lost control of my anger and I don't know for how long.
The bomb has gone off.

Life Is What You Make It
January 19, 1999

Life is what you make it into.
I use to think life was nothing just another mistake.
One man made a difference.
He cared for me.
Not my body just me.
His name is Dalton.
He is really nice.
I thought I was dreaming I had to pinch myself to check
    that I wasn't.
We got married on July 20, 1996 at 2:00pm,
I was 16 he was 31.
We had a little girl,
her name is Evelyn Maryanne Francis.
Before Dalton and I started going out I use to try and kill
    myself.
Since our daughter was born I got out of trying to kill
    myself.
Evelyn turns two on the 27th of this month.
We have been fighting for two years to get her back and it
    don't,
Look that good.
I don't know what I will do if we lose her,
I don't know if
Dalton will stay with me or not,
I do know if I lose Evelyn
I Will need a two or three day watch on me,
But for now I will,
Stay the way I am.
I love you, Evelyn

Does It Mean?
March 24,2000
Age 20

Does it mean anything when I say I love you?
Does it mean anything when I only want you?
Does it mean anything when I look upon the sky and see
    no end?
Do my words mean anything to you?
Do I mean anything to you?
Do you think I'm a keeper?
Does he care what I think?
Does it mean anything when I speak my mind?
Does it mean anything when I speak my feelings?

Feelings Within Feelings
May 2, 2000

Some people say it's good to have feelings within
     feelings.
I know different.
The strongest feeling within a feeling is that I have is hate.
I know hate is a powerful word.
The things I hate are what is within me and out.
I do not like anything within me or out because I hate the
     way
That I am and he way I look.
I hate who I am and who I have become.
I feel that I am a slave to this world.

Breakdown
May 2, 2000

The words break down has so many meanings
But for me,
It means lose control,
Let it all out.
If I lose control who will be my shelter?
Who will keep me in control when I do not feel safe?
I cannot control my actions.
I hope I will not do something stupid when I break down.

Where Do I Belong?
May 10, 2000

Where do I belong? I do not know.
Do I belong here?
Do I belong at moms?
Do I belong at grandmas?
I do not know where I belong anymore.
I do not fit in anywhere I go.
This is how I feel this is how this is who I am.
I do not belong somewhere but it's hard to be I guess.
So I still,
Ask myself where I belong.
And still stay I do not know,
Because I don't.
Someday I will fit in and belong.

What's Holding Me Back?
Jun 12, 2000

As I look out of the window and see everything go by I
    ask,
Myself why I stay in this town there's nothing here for me
    now,
There are no strings holding me back.
So why do I stay.
The only thing in this town worth staying is my
    grandmother.
What's holding me back?
Holding me back from leaving.
Should I or should I not?

My Mind
June 17, 2000

As I open and close the knife thoughts are running
        through my mind.
I do not know why I'm even considering it.
I even started to see things again.
 My mind is telling me all these things and it's hard not to
        listen.
I want to listen but I don't.
My mind is so confusing.
What will I do?
I don't even know any more.

Should I or should I not.

The Dark Side

April 13, 2001
Age 21

I feel that I over stayed my life, that I am passed a due
        date or,
Something.
I've been thinking of the good side of life and the dark side
        of,
My life.
And the dark side of me is stronger and it feels as if the
        dark,
Side of me is taking over me.
For the first time I can't find a reason to fight it.

The Sunset Wave
2001

As I sit down by the water to watch the sun go down,
And to listen to the waves come in and brush along the
    side of the earth.
The waves move so gracefully and quietly.
I wish I could sit here forever.
I like how it's so peaceful.
I wish I was water and be able to move so graceful and
    peaceful.

What Does the Night Breeze
and the Graceful Water Mean?
2001

Listening to the waves brush up on the earth,
And watching the light flicker onto the water that moves
        so,
Gracefully and peaceful.
As I look up from the water and look around me I hear the,
Sounds of the night and I feel the night air upon my face,
And I can see the breeze blow gracefully onto the surface
        of the,
Earth,
And on the water as the breeze makes the water move
        gracefully.
I look upon the shine on the water that the light reflects
        upon the,
Water.
That is what the night breeze and the graceful water is
        about.
Being peace with one's self.

Life, What Is It?

July 22, 2001

What does the word life mean?
To have a life are you not supposed to have someone to
    show,
For it? What is life when you have nothing to show for it?
Does life mean a waste of time when you have nothing to
    show,
For it? I think so.
Life is worth nothing when you have nothing to show for it.
The only thing I have to show is a trial of crumbs.
Isn't life supposed to be full of joy and happiness?
If so then, why is half of the population in this world
    suffers,
From sadness?
Ninety present of my life was and is full of sadness,
The other ten present is happy for I have given my
    daughter a,
Change in life,
So she will have a better life then what I could give her.
Life what is it?
What does it mean?
Is life a good thing or a bad thing to have?
I don't have the answers for all these questions.
I don't think no one has the answers.

A Black Hole From Within
July 27, 2001

A black hole has surfaced within me.
I do not know show it for I need to be strong.
I don't know why I have to be strong.
But I will be strong because I have to.
A black hole from within me is there but no clue why it
     has,
Surfaced.
My gut tells me to dig through it to see what it's made of
     but my,
Mind tells me to fear it.
What to do I do not know.
When I will know I have no clue.

Tears
July 29, 2001

My heart and eyes fill with tears.
My mind is telling me to let them fall down my face.
But if I do that I will be weak and if I do that the blind lady
     will,
Get stronger than what she is now.

Friends

August 14, 2001

There are two kinds of friends.
Good friends that will be there through thick and thin.
They will lend you a shoulder to lean on.
They are there to believe in you.
When you need someone to run to you can always run to
 them.
If you're sad they will try and put a smile on your face.
Their ears are always open.
The best thing of having good friends is they care about
 you.
The secant kind of friends are the bad ones.
They talk good about you when you are around but as
 soon as,
You are gone they start talking bad about you behind your
 back.
They basically stab you in your back.
I am so glad that I have good friends, without them I
 would be,
Lost.
Thank you, God, for really good friends.

Staff No Friends Yes
August 18, 2001

Staff is a title.
But I do not use that title.
I use friends or family,
Because that's what I think of them.
They are more of a family then staff.
They are there to help you when you need them.
It may be their job,
but they think of us as family and that's how,
I think of them,
Good Doesn't Mean Nothing Until You Almost.

Lose What You Have
August 17, 2001

It feels like I have looked at this world for the first time.
It feels like I have just opened my eyes for the first time.
I have realized I have some good things going for me.
And I want more good things going for me.
I am not going to say I am going to do this or not.
Instead I want good things to go for me.
I want to finish school. I want to take a freelance writing
    course.
And become a writer and write novels or poem books.
What I want now is to change my life right around.
I want no I am going to.
I want the help I want to change.
I want my life to be meaningful.
I want a life.

My First Full Day with My New Eyes
August 18, 2001

As I look upon this world I have found a new me.
I know what I want in life and I plan on going for it.
I will finish school.
I will become a freelance writer.
How I know this stuff you ask?
Well because I want it I deserve it.
I am smart enough, and I can do it.
I want my life to be worth something?
To have something to show for it.
I want it bad enough there for I can do it.

Looking Around Me
August 20,2001

I'm not one that usually judges people.
But now I can't help it.
When I look around me and see people who have asked
    for help,
And now they there are people around and people willing
    to help,
Them.
They take time off.
Well I am here to get help.
Last time I was playing around but this time I will not play,
Around.
I want the help.
It is a sign that I was allowed to come back.
I want and will change my life around.
I can feel my life has started to change already.
I thank my good and positive friends.
(Staff) without them I don't think I would have come this
    far,
The staff are my angels that I asked for.
Thank you, God.

Life Now with Meaning

August 21, 2001

My life now has meaning.
Even though it's small but in time it will grow.
I use to think that my life was a mistake and meaningless,
And now I think wow my life is not a mistake and I have,
Meaning to life.
I am good enough to have a meaningful life.
I am starting to do something to show for it.
I am so proud of myself.
I have a strong feeling that I never had before it's called
      pride.
I am beginning to love myself for who I am for the first
      time in,
Twenty one years of my life.
I can't thank my angels enough, but I will make them
      proud of,
Me.
I will succeed in life.

Proud and Pride
August 23, 2001

I am very proud of myself for the way I have started to
     change
My life around.
I have pride in my life.
I am proud of the progress I have and making in my life.
I am proud that my life has started going down the right
     path.
I love the pride I have within myself.
That my life has started going down the right path.
I love the pride I have with myself.
I am beginning to love myself.
My self-esteem is growing.
I love it.

Trust
August 25, 2001

Trust is not something you can buy or take.
Trust is something you earn.
If someone says to you I can trust you than you should be
     proud,
Of yourself that you have earned that person's trust.
I trust my good friends.
They are honest.
If they have something to say to you,
Whether it's good or bad,
They will say it.
If they trust you enough to tell you something private,
That means they trust you not to tell anyone.
If you lose some ones trust it is because you've broken
     their trust.
And it is hard to earn it back.
It is harder to earn the trust back then when you first
     earned it.
I have trust in my good friends,
And I hope they have trust in me.
Trust is not one to lose.

Love
September 2, 2001

Love means more than simply saying I love you.
Love is an emotion that comes from the heart.
Love:
Standing next to the one you claim to love through thick
    and thin.
Listening to the one you love even if you don't
    understand.
Lending a shoulder to your lover to cry upon.
Another kind of love is being a good friend.
Love:
To give a shoulder to lean on.
An open ear when needed.
Being there when a friend is in need.
Love means more than simply saying,
I love you.

Moods of Music
September 12, 2001

Music of all kinds are like moods.
You have the blues and jazz.
You have upbeat music.
You have relaxation music.
All these different kinds of music can go with human
     emotions,
Like sadness,
Happiness,
And even uptight.
All these are moods that music can help with some way or
     another.
If I feel like crying than I put on music that goes with my
     mood.
If I am happy I will put on upbeat music that goes with my
     mood.
If I am up tight or need to relax than I will put on relaxation
     music that goes with my mood.
Music is like meditation but for the soul.
I love my music and I love how it helps my moods,
No matter what mood I am in.

Will Power From Within

September 23, 2001

I have found the will power within myself.
It has taken me a lot of years to find it,
And now that I have it I will not let go of it.
I have the will power to change my life around to the right
    path.
I have the will power to do something with my life.
I have the will power to will.
I have found the will power to live my life to the limit and
    beyond.
I have the will power to say hay I can and will stop hurting
    myself.
I am better than that and always will be better than that.
I have found the will power within me.

Positive Role Models
November 11, 2001

I have always hung around with negative role models ever
        since
I was six years old.
When I found a positive role model I was scared,
Because I did not know what to do,
Or how to act.
That was back in 1995,
Now in 2001 I am not scared of positive role models.
I have a lot of positive role models I consider as family.
I just hope I can hold on to them and they will never lose
        their,
Confidence in me

Why Do I Self Harm?
February 2, 2002

When I first started to hurt myself it was just small
    scratches.
As the years went on I found myself hurting myself more,
And a little worse each time.
It became a copping skill for me.
Every time I was mad or upset,
And did not want to deal with realty,
I would pick up a nail,
Tack,
Or even glass,
Just so I could get my mind off,
Of my emotional pain.
For the last six years I have been to the point of cutting
    myself,
And watch the blood flow,
From where I have cut.
Since I have learned the saying,
" have to swim half way to get the help"
I have finally realized that I have swam half way,
And that it is not those who want to help me that pull
    away,
It's me.
Because all I have ever known how to deal with my
    problems,
Is by cutting myself.
Every time someone has reached out their hand for me,
I pull away.
Because I am scared.
Scared of new things.
The only way I can get the help I need is to not pull back.
Just reach and grab,
The hand that is waiting for me.

One Drop of Blood
November 8, 2002
Age 22

As tears fill my eyes I find it hard to cry,
For I have many tears,
And many reasons to cry.
I have not harmed myself since May.
But the urge is there.
Now more than ever.
One drop of blood is all I want.
So I can relief some stress.
I know people think it's wrong or stupid but I do not.
One drop of blood.

Lonely Again
January 15, 2003

Here I am again.
Feeling alone when I should not.
Baring a child, it feels that no one but me cares about.
Feels like I'm doing this alone with no help.
Am I a real person?
Or is someone making me up?
Do I have to do this alone?
I will if I have to.
Everyone is acting like and making me feel I am all alone.
It feels like no one wants to be a part of my life.
No one is truthful to me.
Everyone is pushing me out of their lives.
So be it.

Why???
February 6, 2003

Why do I put myself in this place of life?
Why do I do what I do?
Why do I live like this?
Why can't things go right for me?
Do I not deserve good things?
Can I have this baby and raise it?
Having a baby and being a mom is two different things.
I gave birth to Evelyn,
But I was not a mom.
It was more like I was her aunt.
Of course I love her as she is my little girl,
And always be.
But don't I deserve to be a mom?
Why?
Why?
Why?

Thinking

February 8, 2003

I have a lot of things to think about.
I do not know if I should get back on my meds.
I do not know if what I am feeling will pass or stay.
I do not know, but I need to know.
Need to know so I can make it through.
Should I ask my doctor about meds I can take?
Do I really need them?
Will I have to change to keep this one?
Should I speak out and say I'm scared?
I know said what needed to be said, but did I do the right
    thing.
These are some of the things I am and need to think
    about.

New? Used?
February 9, 2003

This little one is new to this world and everything and
	everyone
Will be new to the baby.
I am used in this world so nothing is new to me.
I may be young,
To some.
But I'm old and used to the world around me.
I hope this little one will always be new,
And never used like me.

Nerves
February 15, 2003

For the last couple of days my nerves have been going.
I think maybe it's because I get pictures of my baby soon.
I don't know.
But either way I stayed in control.
Today I locked myself out of my room three times today.
I hope my nerves stop going soon.

Moods
February 19, 2003

My moods are not under control anymore.
I am getting sadder by the minute.
Although I don't look like I'm sad, it's because I'm so use
    to,
Hiding it so no one can see.
Sometimes I don't know why I am sad.
It could be because of the abuse i've been through since I
    was 5,
I don't know.
It could be because I don't talk about how I feel.
I don't know.
No one knows how much I really suffered and no one will
    know.
I am both a victim and a server for life.
So it's that why I'm sad or is it more?
I don't know.

The Unknown
May 1, 2003

I do not know if I am allowed to keep the baby that's
        growing,
Within me.
If I lose the baby will I go back to my old ways?
Will I stay the way I am?
Will I be able to live alone?
Will I be able to trust myself?
Do I stand alone or is there someone watching over me?
These are the things that things that are unknown to me.

My Baby
May 20, 2003

When I feel you move inside me, it brings me joy.
Although I do not know if you are a boy or a girl I love you.
I put in your sisters letter that she is going to be a big
     sister.
Your big sister is six years old.
She does not live with mommy, but I never stopped loving
     her,
And never will.
The same thing goes for you.

Rain Fall
May 13, 2003

A rain fall is following me around everywhere I go.
It follows me if I'm inside or outside.
The rain falls all around my body.
Each drop is how I am feeling.
Feelings of sadness,
Scared,
Alone,
A failure,
And hurt.
Each feeling has its own drop of rain,
But always falls together.
I need to find my safe place,
So the rain fall cannot follow me.
I need to lose this rain fall before it turns into a storm,
That I cannot control.
I am not at peace with myself.

First Time Mom Again
September 1, 2003

I am a mother of two.
I have a six year old,
And a two month old,
And it feels like I am a first time mother,
Again.
But in a way I am,
I did not get to raise my six year old,
So to me some things are new,
Others are not.
I think if I did raise my six year old,
I would feel the same way.
Same with other people,
That feel the same way I do.
Maybe because having another baby,
Means something new,
Than when you had your first baby.
This does not mean I love one less than the other,
I love them both the same.
I do not,
Would not
 Play favourites.
I would not in my life time do harm to my children.
If I had to choose my life or theirs,
I would chose my life.
And that's no lie.
My girls are my life.
I would do anything to keep them out of harm's way.
I would put myself in harm's way first.
As a mother of two,
One six and one two months,
 This is how I truly feel.
I might make mistakes sometimes,
But everyone does,
It's called being human.

Cold Hearted???
October 26, 2003

What is cold hearted mean?
Everyone says,
It's when you close your heart,
And don't let anyone in.
Or you fear to feel emotions.
Well I'm both.
I don't want any "adults" in,
I don't want to feel my emotions.
I fear my emotions.
I've been cold hearted for so long,
I don't know how I should feel,
Or when to feel,
Or how to let people know how I feel,
Or that I do feel emotions.
If someone asks me to write,
How I feel,
I can do it,
But ask me to show it I get scared.
Ask me to read it out loud ,
I cannot do it.
Some people tell me,
That something is wrong with me,
Since I don't feel anything.
All I know is yes in a way,
 I am cold hearted,
I admit to it.

Alone
November 20, 2003

I am alone.
I go out to see friends,
But I come home and,
I am alone with my thoughts again.
 If I would scream no one would hear.
Everyone says you're not alone,
But when it's just me…
I am alone.
I am not use to being alone.
Everyone said,
If you need me for anything,
I'm just a phone call away.
What if…
That the phone was out of reach?
What if…
What if I was not me?
At night I feel lost,
Because of how alone I feel.
I am in a box with just enough holes to breathe,
And no way out.
Alone is when I do not know what are my real thoughts,
And what are not my real thoughts…
What is me,
And what is not me.
It's hard to tell what's what when I'm alone.
I will not lie,
I am scared,
When I am alone.
What if…
I was not me?

Maze
2004

My life is a maze.
When I turn a corner it's a straight path.
But after walking it for a while it starts to zig zag.
I went around a zag
Now and it's a dead end.
I've tried to walk back the same way,
But I keep hitting dead ends.
I'm lost in my own maze,
And I don't see a way out.
There's a mirror in my maze,
And every time I pass it and look
I see my mask getting bigger,
And something inside me getting stronger.
I'm ready to scream as loud as I can.
I'm ready to cave in.
I'm scared.

Want
February 25, 2004

All of my emotions want out.
I am scared of them.
Scared because of what I might do to myself,
And the ones I care about.
Already I find myself having these little blow ups.
I don't know why I have these little blow ups,
Until after I do so.
I want out of this box that I put myself in.
I want to scream out loud,
I want to cry.
But I don't want to disappoint anyone.
I don't want anyone to look at me different,
Or act different around me.
Yes I look normal on the outside,
But I do not feel normal on the inside.
I feel like a freak,
Every part of me inside and out.
I want to tell someone how hard it is,
Not to pick up a razor and push down on my wrist,
That every time I pass the bathroom,
I want to pick up a razor,
And run where no one will find me.
The feeling of being half empty without my children,
And without them half of me wants to die.
No one knows how hard,
I'm trying to keep my life on this path.

A Stranger?
February 29, 2004

A stranger in the world around me.
A stranger in my own family.
A stranger in my own body.
A stranger in the mirror looking back at me.
A stranger writing on my paper.

This is what I feel like in side:
The pain I feel,
The suffering,
And the emptiness within me.
This is not a stranger in my life.
Happiness is a stranger to me that I am learning about,
Real happiness.
Motherhood is a stranger to me.
Life is a stranger.
Feeling bad is not a stranger to me.
Wanting to be dead is not a stranger to me.

A stranger in the world around me.
A stranger in my own family.
A stranger in my own body.
A stranger in the mirror looking back at me.
A stranger writing on my paper.
This is what I feel like inside.

Am I?
April 27, 2004
Age 24

Am I alive in side?
Am I cold hearted as been told?
Am I just an empty body?
Am I holding back on propose?
Am I the cause of my own pain?

It does feel like I am dying inside.
It does feel like I am cold hearted.
It does feel like I am an empty body.
It does not feel like I am hold back on propose.
It is unknown if I cause my own pain.

I need to find away to let some out.
I've tried to cry but I can't.
I've tried talking but cant.
There's only one thing left for me to do before list.
If it does not help than I don't know.

Why Not?
2004

As I look out my window and listen to music,
I'm thinking why.
Why can I not cry?
Why can I not feel upset?
Why can I not get mad?
Why can I not feel anything at all?
Why am I so dead inside?
Why can I not pick up a razor and push it down.
Why do I care about disappointing everyone?
Why do I have to get out of bed?
Why do I have to eat?
Why not pick up a razor take it apart and push down?
What do I have to lose?

Why do I not want to go outside?
Why do I even bother?
Why is this happening again?

I Don't Not Want
2004

I do not want to get out of bed.
I do not want to disappoint anyone.
My thoughts and dreams are the same.
I do not want to think.
I do not want to sleep.
I cannot talk about it.
I cannot face it all.
Urge is getting stronger.
I am fighting as hard as I can.
I do not want to get out of bed.
I do not want to disappoint anyone.
My thoughts and dreams are the same.
I do not want to think.
I do not want to sleep.
I cannot talk about it.
I cannot face it all.

I Do Not Know Anymore
September 4, 2004

I do not know who I am anymore.
I do not know if I even exist.
I do not know if I am just a dream.

I know I am not me, I can feel it.
I know I exist to someone.
I know I am in someone's dream.

I do not know if I deserve anything.
I do not know if I deserve anyone.
I do not know if I deserve to live.

I know I don't deserve any of the above.

I do not know who I am anymore.
I do not know if I even exist.
I do not know if I am just a dream.

Pissed Off
September 4, 2004

Pissed off is how I feel.
Pissed off at family.
Pissed off at some friends.
Pissed off at myself.
Pissed off at the world.
Pissed off is how I feel.
I want to vent on my family.
I want to vent on some friends.
I want to vent on myself.
I want to vent on the world.
Pissed off is how I feel.
I need to vent on something before I blow.
Pissed off is how I feel.
Pissed off at family.
Pissed off at some friends.
Pissed off at myself.
Pissed off at the world.

Invisible
September 8, 2004

Am I invisible to my family?
Am I invisible to my lover?
Am I invisible to the world?

Yes I am invisible to my family.
Yes I am invisible to my lover.
Yes I am invisible to the world.

No one hears my cry.
No one hears my voice.
No one hears my heart.

No one will hear my pain.
No one will hear my thoughts.
No one will hear me break.

Don't Want To!!!
September 19, 2004

Don't want to be used anymore!
Don't want to be a victim anymore!
Don't want to live anymore!
Don't want to be the black sheep anymore!

This is what I want.
This is how I feel.
This is what I think.

Don't want to be used anymore!
Don't want to be a victim anymore!
Don't want to live anymore!
Don't want to be the black sheep anymore!

Too Good To Be True
September 26, 2004

He is too good to be true.
I feel as if I am forever dreaming.
For the way he treats me no on in my whole life has done.
He makes me feel like I am a someone and not a nobody.
He taught me so much.
He has taught me that I am not a mat for everyone to walk
    on.
He has taught me that I am worth something more than a
    mat,
A pushing bag and a lay.
Sometimes I pinch myself,
To see if I am dreaming,
Because it feels too good to be true.
The way I feel when I am with him,
I have never felt before.
Sometimes I feel like I don't deserve him and that he can
    do better,
But then he says I love you,
And that feeling goes away.
When I hear him say I love you,
It sounds real,
That it comes from his heart,
And that he's just not saying it to get in my pants.
I have never felt like this before.
He is too good to be true.
But he is true and real.

Sleepless Nights
October 7, 2004

I can't sleep at night no more.
Even though my eyes are heavy as can be.
It's not that I am not tired,
Because I am very tired.
I lay in my bed,
Nice and snug,
Eyes closed,
Yet I cannot sleep.
I do not know why.
I'll be lucky that one of my sleeping pills will work.
Is it because my mind is on over time?
I can't stop thinking,
I can't clear my mind like I use to.
I want to grab a razor so bad,
But I don't want to disappoint dad,
Bill or Marina.
So I will continue to fight the urge.
I don't know for how long,
But I will fight it as long as I can.
I don't know how many more sleepless nights,
Are ahead of me,
I wish I knew.
I want dad,
Bill,
And Marina,
To know that it's not them,
It's me,
Something is wrong with me,
And I don't know what or,
Even why.

The Feeling
October 20, 2004

The feeling I have,
Has been building for a while now.
I've been fighting it the whole time.
I don't know if I can fight it anymore.
Thoughts are racing through my head.
I so want to do it.
So much is on my mind,
That I would not know where to even begin,
To tell anyone my racing thoughts.
I want to do what's normal,
For me to do when this happens.
I can see myself doing it in my mind.
But that's not helping.
Seeing it in my head makes me want to do it more.
And in a way,
I don't want fight this feeling any more.
I just want to do it.
Pick up a razor and take it across my arm.
I don't care how small or big or even how deep.
I just want to do it.

Break
November 15, 2004

I feel like I am going to break.
Break into tears and cry until I have no tears left.
Break down and let the "bomb" go off.
Let people know what's really going on within me.
Break so bad that I just want to die.
Why do I feel like I am going to break?
Well for one I feel that I do not belong here or anywhere.
I feel as if I am a chip on everyone's shoulder.
I feel as I need to break.
Break in all ways.
I feel so…
So…
I don't know how right now.

Falling
November 20, 2004

It feels as if I am falling down a hole.
If I look up I no longer see the sunlight.
If I look down I can see the bottom.
But I cannot tell when I'll land.
All around me as I fall,
I can see my thoughts taking place,
As if they were happening.
It feels as if I am falling down a hole.
I do not know what kind of hole it is,
Or even if I'll stop falling.
It feels as if I am falling down a hole.
There is nothing to grab to stop from falling.
What to do…
I do not know.

Losing
December 6, 2004

I am losing control of my thoughts.
I am slowly losing control of my actions.
I am losing all control.
I've been losing control for a while.
I've been fighting so much to keep in control.
But nothing seems to be working anymore.
It feels like I don't have control of nothing right now!!!
I can't snap out of this.
I don't remember the last time I was like this.
I mean before I could snap out of this within a day.
But now I can't seem to snap out of it at all.
And I'm getting mentally tired of fighting.
I feel so helpless.
I know my love is trying so hard to help me,
And I keep telling him that,
I'm sorry,
That I am like this,
And that it has nothing to do with him.
But I know since I've been like this
It's hurting him so much.
But I don't know if I'll ever snap out of this.
Seeing him hurting because of me,
Breaks my heart.
Maybe…
Maybe he deserves better.

I am losing control of my thoughts.
I am slowly losing control of my actions.
I am losing all control.

Thoughts
December 10, 2004

As I lay on my bedroom floor,
My mind starts to wonder.
I start to think of one day,
I will be able to spend Christmas with my daughters again.
But then,
I think of my grandmother,
So many thoughts,
Like how I did not get to say goodbye,
The fact that I didn't see her for about a month before she
        died.
And now I'll never be able to see her again.
Why do people have to die?
Why can't I be dead too?
Why do I feel like I want to lock myself in a room,
And never come out?
Why do I even fight my thoughts anymore?
I just want to hide in a corner,
With a razor and press it along my wrist,
So I can that pain instead of feeling,
What I do right now.
That urge is so strong.
And I don't want to fight it anymore.
God forgive me
I don't want to fight that urge,
Anymore.

Tic Tok
December 16, 2004

Tic tok the clock starts to count down.
Tic tok my temper will blow.
Tic tok my blood starts to over boil.
Tic tok I'm going to blow.

Time is running out
I can't keep control much longer.
I don't want to keep control anymore.
I just want to haul off and punch something,
Or something else.

Tic tok the clock starts to count down.
Tic tok my temper will blow.
Tic tok my blood starts to over boil.
Tic tok I'm going to blow.

Christmas
December 30, 2004

Christmas has passed,
Yet nothing has changed,
When it comes to how I feel.
Which is a bit worse than I was about a month ago.
Some things have gotten worse,
As in feeling sad,
It has increase.
B.L has gotten hard to control.
My nightmares are getting worse.
Even sometimes I'll dream the same one,
Two nights in a row.
I feel as if I am losing everything.
I know I hurt some people when I hurt myself,
But the urge is getting real strong and I know,
B.L can feel that to.
And the reason for it getting stronger,
Is because I feel as if I let my girls down,
And my grandma.
I miss them all so much.
Christmas was really hard to go through,
Without them.
I know I will be able to spend Christmas with my girls,
One day.
And I know grandma is always around,
In spirit.
But I am finding that I am having trouble,
Keeping awake,
And I think that's because,

I don't want to wake up.
I don't want to eat,
I don't want to look into a mirror,
I don't want to even drink anything.
But I force myself to do those things.
What am I going to do?
I don't have a fucking clue.

Falling Back Down
January 6, 2005

I need to release.
I need to vent.
I need to do it soon.

I'm falling back down again.
It feels like I am falling farther than before.
Thoughts racing through my mind,
Yet it's a blank.
Staying in control is getting harder to do.
Writing is getting hard to do.
The urge is the hardest to fight,
I know that I will hurt the ones I love.
But I don't know how much longer,
I can fight it.
I don't mean to hurt them.
I'm falling back down,
Again.
It feels like I am falling,
Farther than before.

I need to release.
I need to vent.
I need to do it soon.

Fear
February 2, 2005

I fear to sleep.
I fear to dream.
I fear to be alone.

Fear is running through my vines.
Fear is running through my mind.

I fear to face the ones who have hurt me.
I fear to remember how they have hurt me.
I do not want to face them.
I do not want to remember how.
I want to hide in a dark room with no windows.
Fear is taking over me.
I am scared.

I fear to sleep.
I fear to dream.
I fear to be alone.

Fear is running through my vines.
Fear is running through my mind.

Lost

February 5, 2005

Lost control of my thoughts.
Lost control of my body.

I have lost all control.
I have lost the fight.
I am no longer in control.
I have lost sight of the light.
I am now lost in the dark.
I am lost in my own mind maze,
And cannot see,
Anything.
Is there a way out of this dark maze?
Can I ever get control back?
Or will I forever be lost?
I don't have an answer for any of them.
I have lost,
All control.

Lost control of my thoughts.
Lost control of my body.

To
February 24, 2005

To push down.
To watch blood flow.
To feel one pain instead of another.

I want to push down and watch the blood flow.
I want to feel one pain instead of another.
I want all of this,
More than before.
I'm all set to do it,
So what's holding me back?
Is it because everyone is awake?
Maybe.
All I know is that I want to do it.
I want to push down.
I need to do this.

To push down.
To watch blood flow.
To feel one pain instead of another.

Wonder What's Next
March 17, 2005
Age 25

As I sit here and look around
I start to wonder what lays ahead,
For me.
Like will I finish my book?
Will I keep Bill happy?
Much more goes through my mind.
But I cannot write them all down.
I am really happy with Bill,
And I am doing real good
Getting my book done.
But right now,
I got writers block.
Even now,
Writing this,
I have,
Writers block.
So I'm putting my pen down
And sit here,
And wonder,
What lays ahead,
For me.

Would You?
April 14, 2005

If I started to cry would you wipe away my tears and tell
     me everything will be ok?
If I was down would you try to lift me up?
If I was scared would you tell me that it's ok?
If I was sick would you be there and take care of me?
If I was dying would you be there?
If I was on my deathbed,
Would you pray for me to get better,
Or would you welcome death to take me?

Got To Hold Back
April 16, 2005

Got to hold back so much.
Got to hold back my pain.
Got to hold back my tears.
Got to hold back my anger.

I got to hold back so much.
And it hurts in so many ways.
I can't even write down,
Everything,
I,
Hold,
Back.
Never mind talking about it.
All that I hold back,
Is bit by bit,
Breaking me.
If I break all the way,
I will lose,
Everything.

Got to hold back so much.
Got to hold back my pain.
Got to hold back my tears.
Got to hold back my anger.

Freak Out
May 24, 2005

I want to freak out.
I want to hit and punch.
I want to vent.
Four days ago my fuse was lit.
I don't know how or why it was lit.
Three days ago it was still burning slow.
I punched something, I don't know why.
Two days ago it was still burning slow,
I punched a few things but harder than the day before.
I fought the urge to punch something and succeeded.
Today it's still burns, but slower,
And I find myself fighting the urge to freak out.
I don't know why I am like this,
I don't know how long I'll be like this.
I just know that I want to freak out so bad.
And if it gets worse than nothing will stop me from
        freaking out.
I want to freak out.
I want to hit and punch.
I want to vent.

Our Time
May 28, 2005

I do not want to sleep.
I want to stay awake.
If I stay awake,
Then he and I can spend some time together,
Just the two of us.
I do not go to bed when I start to get tired,
Just because,
I'll miss our alone time,
Even if it's just for a second.
I do not want to miss our alone time.
Since we have moved,
We only have had our alone time when it's bedtime.
I miss our time together.
If I went to sleep when I get tired,
Then I'll miss our time.
And I do not want to miss it.
I want to cry because I miss him so much.
Even if he is sitting right next to me.
I love him so much.
And I don't think I can tell him enough.
But I miss our alone time.

The Storm
June 18, 2005

It's calm before the storm.
The storm is getting closer.
It feels like there is a volcano inside of me,
Getting ready to erupt.
I can feel it running through my veins.
I can feel the storm cloud getting heavier over my head.
When this storm hits,
I don't even want to be here.
I don't want to be.
Because I will lose everything,
And everyone,
In my life.
And I don't know how I will handle it.
This storm is scaring me.
But I don't know if it's preventable.
If it is,
I can't seem to find it.
And would I find it,
Before the storm is here?
I just want to run and hide from everything,
And everyone,
So when the storm is here,
I might not lose anything.
I know where to run,
But I don't know if I should or not.
Part of me does want to run.
I don't know what to do anymore.
This storm is messing,
With my mind.

Snap
July 20, 2005

I feel so lost.
I feel so alone.
I feel half dead.
I feel like I'm going to snap.

I am lost in my mind.
I can't tell if I am coming or going.
I feel so alone,
Because I feel so ugly,
On the outside,
And on the inside.
I don't know why anyone wants to be close to me.
Family or not.
I feel half dead inside,
I really want to vent,
Just so I can feel like I'm alive.
It's been months since I vented.
But it's been on my mind a lot lately.
I feel like I'm going to snap in more than one way.
I feel like I'm going to snap at everyone around me.
I feel like I'm going to snap mentally.
Worse than ever before.

I feel so lost.
I feel so alone.
I feel half dead.
I feel like I'm going to snap.

Baby Sister
2005

Baby sister the one to get picked on.
Baby sister always the worry wart.
Baby sister that I sometimes get jealous of.
Baby sister the one I thought I was going to lose.
I love you so much.
Sorry for all the things I have done to you.
Please forgive me baby sister.
I never knew how much I care for you until I thought I was
        going to lose you.
I love you baby sister.

Mother Wanted
July 26, 2005

All I wanted was to be loved by her.
All I wanted was to be accepted by her.
All I wanted was to be told I was wanted by her.
All I wanted was to be believed by her.

She has my unconditional love.
She has my acceptance.
She has my belief in her.
She is wanted by me.

All I want is to be loved by her.
All I want is to be accepted by her.
All I want is to be wanted by her.
All I want is to be believed by her.

All I wanted and still want is my
MOTHER.

This Feeling
September 23, 2005

I feel really strange inside.
So strange that I do not,
Know,
What I'm feeling.
This feeling I don't have a name for.
This feeling came on all of a sudden.
I don't know what's going on inside of me.
I do know I don't like it.
And that it scares me.
I don't know when I'll snap out of it.
But I hope soon.
But until I do,
I will put a smile on my face,
And hope no one sees,
Through it.

Grandma
October 8, 2005

When I think of grandma,
I think of Graceful Respected Apple pies,
Nice Discipline Mother,
 And awesome.
I also think of unconditional love.
These are the things that I think about,
When I think of my grandma.
I miss her so much.
Sometimes I wish I was with her.
She was more than my grandma,
She was like a mother to me.
She always listened to me,
Even if I was making no sense.
She always had her ears ready,
To hear what I had to say.
Every little thing reminds me of her.
All I have left of her,
Is my memories.
But I will never forget,
And I will never stop loving her.
She is and always will be,
A part of me.
Even though she is gone,
I hope I still make her proud of me.
And I hope wherever she is,
She is happy.
Oh grandma,
I love you so much,
And I miss seeing you.
I will never forget you,
And I hope one day,
We will be together again.

Blank

November 6, 2005

Blank is my mind.
Blank is my emotions.
Blank is my body.
I feel so blank, like a blur.
I don't feel a thing yet I feel everything.
I feel like I am in quick sand, but at the same time I feel,
Like my feet are in a cement block.
Everything moving so fast that it's all blank.
Yet moving so slowly that it's a blur.
I have never been like this before as I can remember.
I don't know if I am coming or going.
I don't know what's what.
I don't know who I am anymore.
I don't know anything anymore.
I feel so blank, like a blur.
Blank is my mind.
Blank is my emotions.
Blank is my body.

Did I?
November 8, 2005

Did I lie?
Did I tell half the truth?
Did I do the right thing?
I only told half the truth.
But at the same time I lied.
Why did he say that when I was going to tell him the
        whole,
Truth.
If I knew what he meant before we began would I have
        told,
Him the truth?
I don't know.
But I do know that all I want to do is hide.
Hide from everyone and everything.
I feel so ashamed. I'm at a lost.
I don't know what I want or do.
Please help, My Lord.
Did I lie?
Did I tell half the truth?
Did I do the right thing?

Locked Up
November 9, 2005

So much inside locked up for no one to know.
Locked because I don't want to fail the ones I love and
     fail,
Dr. Sharma. Everyone thinks I'm doing well,
And that how I have come so far over the years.
For them to know how close I came yesterday it would,
Disappoint them so much. I feel so ashamed.
I feel am a frailer whether or not they know.
What's wrong with me?
Why do I do this to myself and the ones I love?
Why do I allow people to love me, and be close to me?
All I do is fail them one way or another, whether or not,
They know it or not.
Why do I keep locking up my emotions?
Why am I so scared of them?
Why do I keep the real truth locked up?
Why do I keep anything locked up?
I can't even write everything that's locked up.
I want to run so bad.
Run so no one will find out how much I'm failing them.
Run so no one will be disappointed by me again.
So much inside locked up for no one to know.

What Am I To Do?
2006

What am I to do?
What am I to say?

I've lost the fight,
And don't know how to follow through.
I'm scared,
Of following through.
Scared,
Of feeling more alone,
Than I do now.
I don't want to argue anymore.
I just want to spend time together,
Do what couples do.
I don't care if they come over for a few hours.
I know I need to make changes,
And help around the house more,
But if I start doing it,
And change,
Will he make the changes he needs to do?
I think we are lost.
We don't talk anymore,
We don't sleep at the same time much.
I don't know what to do.

What am I to do?
What am I to say?

Purify and Purge
March 7, 2006
Age 26

Purify and purge my body,
Purify and purge my insides,
Purify and purge my life,
On my mind purify and purge.
Over and over again for days now.
Look in the mirror and see an ugly stranger looking back,
At me.
A voice saying purge all you consume.
Louder with every passing day, purge what you consume.
My mind telling me to listen to the voice.
Maybe I will maybe I won't.
I don't know yet.
Purify and purge my body,
Purify and purge my insides,
Purify and purge my life.

Whispers
May 27, 2006

Words whispered in my ears yet no one around to
     whisper.
Can't tell what's real and what's not.
I'm trapped in two lives.
I'd rather be in one life instead of the other one.
One where there is no pain of any kind.
I know how to get to that life and stay in it.
And got the means to do so.
An all most the will to do it.
I'm lost in the fog.
Whispers all around me.
Don't know where they are coming from.
Sometimes louder, sometimes can barely hear the
     whispers but,
It's always there.
Day by day it gets harder to fight.
It's getting hard to say no to the whispers and to call upon
     the,
Sandman to take me forever.

Words

August 20, 2006

Words that need to be spoken,
But will not leave my tongue.
Words that only can be written.
But need to be spoken for my mind to be at ease.
How to get these words off my tongue?
I do not know.
If not spoken the urge will come back and all will not be
    good.
All will build up again and the rock will break down again.
Rain falls building up slowly some will fall but even then
    words,
Might not make it off my tongue.
Must force these words out?
And if I do would be taken from me my words.
All of them or bits and pieces?
How can I speak these words to make them
    understandable?
I'm at a loss for spoken word but have gained back my
    writing,
Words.
But I need to speak these words for my mind to be at
    ease.

This Thing Called Life
January 14, 2007

This thing called life I don't want anymore.
This thing called life I want to give up on.
This thing called life I want to give away.
This thing called life is a waste.
This thing called life please take it back.
This thing called life is too much to take it anymore.
This thing called life I don't want anymore.

Messed Up
May 25, 2007
Age 27

Messed up thoughts.
Messed up emotions.
Messed up mind.
I've been messed up for going on months.
Racing thoughts that are no good and one I have acted
    on,
That no one knows about.
My emotions are messed up, mood swings are often and
    more,
Uncontrollable.
My mind is messed up; it's telling me that I should not
    trust,
Anyone.
I don't know who to turn to so I go uptown and sit to write
    and,
Think.
Sometimes it helps other times it makes everything worse.
I am so messed up.
I don't know what to do.
Messed up thoughts.
Messed up emotions.
Messed up mind.

All Whys
June 24, 2007

Why does it have to be this way?
Why did I end up like this?
Why did I have to be born?
Why is it that whenever I think things are changing for the
    better,
They don't?
Why don't I have a back bone so I can say what's on my,
Mind?
Why am I that does everything wrong?
Why should I hope for the best when I know it will never,
Happen?
Why do I let everything and everyone get to me?
Why do I still make myself get out of bed every day?
Why is this the only path for me?
Why do I even try to change knowing i'll just end up like
This again?
Why do I stay alive?
Why do I continue to write when it does not help
    anymore?
Why do I think I can write a book that will help others,
When I can't even say that I have overcome everything?
Why is there all of these whys and more?

Calm Waves

October 2, 2007

Calm waves is me.
Calm waves is my mind.
Calm waves is my body.
Calm waves are my moods.
I am as calm as can be now that I am on meds again.
No more racing thoughts that should not be.
No more bad bad aches and pains.
No more swings of moods.
I am as calm as can be now that I am on meds again.
Calm waves is me.
Calm waves is my mind.
Calm waves is my body.
Calm waves are my moods.

Sober
October 28, 2007

Sober for a year,
Sober I try to stay.
It's been a year since my last drink.
It's been a long and hard year.
I've been tested over the year to have one drink but did
    not take.
The craving to take goes up and down but not as strong
    as,
It is today.
No one to turn to in this time of need.
Must fight craving alone.
Sober for a year prude of myself I am.
But fighting the craving alone I must is hard to do.
For in this time of need there is no one to turn to.
Strong need to be for this craving will to pass.
Sober for a year,
Sober I try to stay.

A Great Storm
March 7, 2008
Age 28

There is a great storm building with in me.
A storm that has everything.
Anger,
Tears,
Urges,
Great sadness,
I want to run and hide.
Run to a place that only I can go.
A place that I can let this great storm out from within me.
A place where no one will hear my screams of anger.
A place where no one will see my tears come out.
A place where no one will see my urges acted on.
A place where no one will see this great sadness upon
    my,
face.
A place where I can let it all out.
A place where this great storm can run its course.
There is a great storm building with in me.
A storm that has everything,
Anger,
Tears,
Urges,
Great sadness.

Aches + Stress – Close Down
March 20, 2008

My body aches everywhere, inside and out.
My body aches in my back,
My body aches in my feet and toes,
My body aches in my legs,
My body aches in my chest,
My body aches in my head.
My body is stressed to near maxed.
My body is stressed to sadness,
My body is stressed to missed monthly,
My body is stressed to aches,
My body is stressed to scream,
My body is stressed to close down.

Father
June 15, 2008

For all the times I was sad,
For all the times I was angry,
For all the times I was hurting,
For all the times I was sick,
For all the times I was in need of a ear,
For all the times I am in need of anything.
You are there for all these times.
Thank you for being my father.
You are my number one DAD.

Can't Take Anymore
July 2, 2008

Can't take this quit anymore,
Can't take this anger anymore,
Can't take this sadness anymore,
Can't take this pain anymore,
Can't take this place anymore,
Can't take this life anymore,
I am done with everyone and everything.
Too much bull shit from every corner of my life.
I have had enough.
I can't take anymore.
I am done!!!
It's not worth It.!!!
Can't take this quit anymore,
Can't take this anger anymore,
Can't take this sadness anymore,
Can't take this pain anymore,
Can't take this place anymore,
Can't take this life anymore.

Remember When?

July 12, 2008

Remember when you baked cookies and cakes you let
    me,
Clean the bowl with my fingers?
Remember when you slapped my hand when you caught,
Me in the cookie jar?
Remember when you made funny faces at me and
    always,
Got me to smile?
Remember when you and I sat on the porch and talked,
About anything as we watched the cars and people go
    by?
Remember when you wrapped my arm up and held my,
Tight until mom and dad got home?
Remember when you hurt your arm and shoulder and I,
Moved in to help you around the house?
I remember everything and how much you loved me.
I will always love and remember you GRANDMA

The Great Storm Is Here
January 31, 2009

The great storm that has been building and coming is
	here.
Over flowing with the great sadness,
The great anger, the great guilt, the great shame,
The great storm,
Is here.
And I have found my way through it.
I am on the right path that will get me through this storm,
And I am walking along it.
Our hearts beat as one now we both can feel it beating.
I am thankful I do not have to walk this path alone this
	time.
Because if I did, I would lose this fight again,
And go back to how I use to be,
And would lose all that I have gained.
The great storm will not win this time.
I am not alone and because of that I will win this fight.

Lost for Words

May 21, 2009
Age 29

In a darken time the light is slowly going out from the path,
I walk.
Feelings of lost and sadness starting to consume me.
Feelings that I cannot do right no matter how hard I try.
I cannot hide my emotions like I use to, old urges coming
     back,
Strong.
No one's fault but my own.
My own because of letting everything build up within.
Expressing myself the only way I know how and good at,
But have lost my words of expressions.
As I write even now I do not truly know what to write.
Without words of my own to write,
Words that are lost I bring,
This to an end.

Hurting
October 9, 2009

Why does it hurt so much?
Why doing something good ends up being a bad thing
    and hurts,
More?
Always letting myself get hurt.
Always trying to be good, and help others but only to get
    burned,
And hurt.
I'm done letting myself get hurt.
I'm done helping others.
Why does it hurt so much?
Why doing something good ends up being a bad thing
    and hurts,
More?

How the Fuck?
January 11, 2011
Age 30

How can people say,
"Ya I know how you feel?" When I don't,
Even know how I feel?
How can people say they understand me when I don't
      even,
Fucking understand myself?
How can people say,
"I'm here for you if you need me," but,
No one is there when you fucking need them?
Fuck there's no one that gets me even if they say they do,
Because I don't even fucking get me?
No one there, no one around me, just me and these
      fucking,
Words and thoughts.
Fuck man I need to vent,
I need to let lose,
Need to release.
Fucking running out of ways,
Running out of time.
How can people say,
"Ya, I know how you feel" when I don't,
Even know how the fuck I feel?

When?

December 13, 2014
Age 34

When I want to call you I can't,
When I want help those with question's I can't,
When I want to reach out and shake some people I can't,
When I want to tell someone to go away and let me deal
    with my own I can't,
My path is getting very dark and what light is left is very
    dime.
Now people will tell me to turn the cant's to can or will, but
    understand this before you tell me either of those two
    things.
There are no phones in heaven,
Not everything has an answer to it,
Shaking someone won't help them or make them see the
    truth,
Family and friends come first and I come last.

What Is Real?
January 24, 2015

What is real?
This life real?
This heart real?
This love real?
This pain real?
This guilt real?
This fear real?
This sadness real?
Am I real?
It's hard to tell anymore what is and what is not real to me.
Things have changed since i found out about the cyst on
    my brain.
I am trying to keep my family and my dear friends close,
But at the same time,
At an arm's length,
So that I do not hurt them.
This is the reason for what is real?

About Time
April 8, 2016
Age 36

It's about time I stop caring what others think of me and
    start thinking of what I think of myself.

Some people may think I am just a lazy dumb person,
Some people may think I am cold hearted,
Some people may think I always get what I want,
Some people may think I non-social,

It's about time I stop caring what others think of me and
    start thinking of what I think of myself.

I am not a lazy dumb person.
There are things that I cannot do no matter how hard I try
    to do them,
Like cooking and the right way to clean my home.
Reason why?
My brain dose not posses things like everyone else's,
Things I learn do not always stick in my memory.

I am not cold hearted.
I do my best to help everyone in my life in any way that I
    can.
I do not get everything I want.
What do I mean?
I want my mom back,
I want my family to always get along,
I want my friends and family to be healthy.
I want to get married to the love of my life.

I am not non-social.
Reasons why?
I have panic attacks when there is a lot going on around
    me,

I have panic attacks when I step outside my front door.
I am a good person,
I am not lazy or dumb.

I am a warm hearted person.
I care for everyone that is in my life
And even those that are not in my life right now.

I am ok with not getting everything I want.
I am doing my best to social and take back control of my
        attacks.

If you are reading this and laughing about it all,
That's fine with me because
I won't let it bring me down.
I will keep my head held high.
I am who I am,
And that is that.

Another Birthday
May 10, 2016

Another Birthday that I cannot call you,
And wish you Happy Birthday,
Another Birthday that I cannot come,
And give you hugs and kisses,
Another Birthday that makes me want to,
Sleep,
It away,
So that I do not cry,
Another Birthday that makes me,
Want to wish that you were here,
And for me to take your place in heaven.
Happy Birthday Mom I hope your dancing with the stars,
Happy Birthday Mom I hope your having a party with
        grandma,
Grandpa and all those that love you,
That now have you to them self's in heaven.

Numb
July 11, 2016

Use to make sure I was numb 24/7,
From when I was 15 years old,
Numb was my copping,
Never wanted to feel hate,
Never wanted to feel anger,
Never wanted to feel alone,
Never wanted to feel grief,
Never wanted to feel any of these so I made myself numb,
Now I am un-numbing myself,
Now I am facing my hate,
Now I am facing my anger,
Now I am facing feeling alone,
Now I am facing grief,
Now I have to learn what one is what all over again,
Now I have to re-teach myself like a child to feel all these
    again,
Lord, please help me.

Sorry
August 17, 2017
Age 37

Sorry if I pushed too much,
Sorry if I made you worried,
Sorry if I tried too hard,
Sorry if I stepped over the line in anyway,
Sorry if I scared you off,
All I have wanted and will always want is to be your friend,
All I ever wanted and prayed for you,
All I have to offer is my friendship and my unconditional
        love for you
That I have had since I felt you kick,
I hope you and I will be more but will not push for it,
I hope and pray that you keep getting all that I wanted for
        you and more,
I hope you will in time be in my life more,
Sorry if I pushed too much,
Sorry if I made you worried,
Sorry if I tried too hard ,
Sorry if I stepped over the line in anyway,
Sorry if I scared you off.

Sorry II
September 21, 2017

Sorry I have done things wrong,
Sorry I upset you,
Sorry I caused you pain,
Sorry I was not there,
Sorry I am a mess,
Sorry I could not be there,
Sorry I did not change a lot of this,
Sorry but I will always love and miss you till my last
    breath,
If I could go back in time to change things that have
    happened,
I would in a heartbeat.

Why, Lord?
January 17, 2018

Why, lord,
Have you not answered my prayers?
Have you written me off?
Are my sins greater,
Than my prayer?
Why have you not answered my prayers
Lord?

Hearts Heavy
March 11, 2018
Age 38

Hearts heavy,
Minds heavy,
Thoughts racing heavy.
Been waiting for years for the day to come and it did last
    year.
But why has it all stopped?
Have I done something wrong?
Have I done too little?
Have I done too much too fast?
All I want is a friendship,
All I want is happiness on all sides,
All I want is to show who I really am,
All I want is to show all you are,
All I want is to be.

Round-About
March 2, 2019

Another turn,
Another bend,
Another break point,
Another round about,
Story of my Life,
Never away out of the line of fire,
Marked for life.
Almost 39,
But why?
Now know how things will be again in two years,
Know always will be the easy target,
Know always will be marked,
Why wait the two years?
Why be marked?
Easy stuck in the endless round about
There is no out,
Stuck for ever at the most inner part,
Of the round a bout,
No place to move,
No place to turn to the next line,
No outs.
Another turn,
Another bend,
Another break point,
Another round about.

My body
March 16, 2019
Age 39

My soul,
My blood,
My breaths,
Life was given twice by these four,
Life that will always be part of me,
Life that I would never want a due over,
Life that I only hope reach's fullest,
Maybe in the next life will be a part of my life,
But I can't hold back the pain anymore.
I wish you both love and long life,
The only gift I could give you both.
Love always,
A childless mother.

I am sorry
August 18, 2020
Age 40

I am sorry I lose things,
I am sorry I am messed up,
I am sorry I am not good enough,
I am sorry I am not all that is needed,
I am sorry I lost the fight,
I am sorry I am a coward,
I am sorry I am so lost,
I am sorry I am nothing,
I am sorry I don't keep some promises,
I am sorry for just being,
I am sorry.

Too Quick To Accept
2020

See everyone is quick to accept others issues.
Our sexuality,
Our lifestyle,
Our hearts,
But as soon as a mental health disorder is said,
All act like they didn't hear,
Or shame the person,
And not believe,
Because they never told before.
But why not tell right off the back about these things?
Fear,
Abandoned,
Not believed,
Hopeless,
Lose all,
For those reasons people suffer in silence,
They don't speak up,
They don't tell,
They carry it hidden,
Under years of masks,
And suppression.
Don't be judgmental to what you don't fully understand,
Or know.
Your words and action can do a few things,
Harm,
Kill,
Or shine a light for someone,
Who is under a mask.

About the Author &:

Linda Westbrook was born March 5, 1980 and raised in Brantford, Ontario, Canada. By all that is right and good, Linda should have had a wonderful, normal childhood of fantasies and sunny days. But this was not the case for Linda.

Linda started suffering sexual abuse at the age of five years old at the hands of two family members. No one seemed to believe what Linda was trying to tell them, not even her mother who allowed the most vicious abuser to continue to visit the home. The abuse continued until the age of 14, when Linda and her little sister were finally removed from the home for their safety.

At the age of seven, Linda began self abuse as a way to cope with the trauma of the abuse. At the age of ten Linda started using cigarettes, alcohol and drugs as a means of escape. Many times Linda tried to end her pain by overdosing on the very pills she was using as an escape. After finally being removed from the home, Linda was first put into a mental health facility for six months to examine the extent of her emotional and physical abuse, then into a group home for another six months. It was here that Linda learned to write and began writing poetry for the first time.

Finally, Linda finally had her day in court. The Judge gave Linda the right to choose whether she wanted to stay in the group home or go back to her family home. Seeing her mother crying in court, Linda opted to go back home, where she stayed for another six months before running away for a month. When she came home, she found her mother and little sister preparing to move. Linda was 15.

Linda had her first child at age 16 and second at age 21. Both children were removed at the hospital out of fear her past abuse history and learning disabilities would make her an unfit parent. She was never given the chance to prove them wrong.

Linda still lives in Canada with her partner of many years. Her life is filled with loved ones near and far, friends, and partners. She met her oldest daughter in 2017. She is now a grandmother.

Linda has Dissociative Identity Disorder, better known as DID, a form of plurality caused by trauma before age nine. She and her alters have learned to work as a team. They face life together.

& *"The many in us recognize the many in you."*